Good For Me
Meat and Fish

Sally Hewitt

WAYLAND

Notes for Teachers and Parents

Good for Me is a series of books that looks at ways of helping children to develop a positive approach to eating. You can use the books to help children make healthy choices about what they eat and drink as an important part of a healthy lifestyle.

Look for meat and fish when you go shopping.
- Look at the different types of meat and fish in your local supermarket.
- Read the ingredients on packets to see if the food contains meat and fish.
- Buy something new. Have fun preparing it and eating it with children.

Talk about different food groups and how we need to eat a variety of food from each group every day.
- Meat and fish are protein. Discuss other kinds of food that are protein.
- Talk about the ways protein helps to keep us strong and healthy.

Talk about how we feel when we are healthy and the things we can do to help us to stay healthy.
- Eat food that is good for us.
- Drink plenty of water.
- Enjoy fresh air and exercise.
- Sleep well.

First published in 2007 by Wayland
Copyright © Wayland 2007
Wayland
338 Euston Road
London NW1 3BH

Wayland Australia
Hachette Children's Books
Level 17/207 Kent Street
Sydney NSW 2000

Produced by Tall Tree Ltd
Editor: Jon Richards
Designer: Ben Ruocco
Consultant: Sally Peters

British Library Cataloguing in Publication Data
Hewitt, Sally, 1949–
   Meat and fish. – (Good for me)
   1. Meat – Juvenile literature 2. Fish as food – Juvenile
literature 3. Health – Juvenile literature
   I. Title
   641.3'6

   ISBN-13: 9780750249997

Printed in China
Wayland is a division of Hachette Children's Books.

Picture credits:
Cover top Alamy/Stock Image, bottom Alamy/Neil Holmes,
1 Dreamstime.com/Bobby Deal, 4 Dreamstime.com,
5 Dreamstime.com/Mikhail Nekrasov, 6 Dreamstime.com,
7 Dreamstim.com/Paul Cowan, 8 Dreamstime.com/Bobby Deal,
9 Getty Images/Stockbyte, 10 Alamy/Neil Holmes,
11 Dreamstime.com/Gordon Logue, 12 Dreamstime.com, 13 Alamy/Doug
Houghton, 14 Dreamstime.com, 15 Tall Tree Ltd, 16 Alamy/Blend Images,
17 Dreamstime.com/Liv Friis-larsen, 18 Dreamstime.com, 19 Alamy/Paul
Felix Photography, 20 middle Corbis, bottom left Dreamstime.com/Arturo
Limon, bottom middle Dreamstime.com, bottom right Dreamstime.com/Liz
Van steenburgh, 21 top middle Alamy/Foods of the World, centre left
Dreamstime.com/Cameron Pashak, upper centre Dreamstime.com/Kutt
Niinepuu, centre right Dreamstime.com, centre Dreamstime.com, bottom
left Dreamstime.com, bottom middle Dreamstime.com, bottom right
Dreamstime.com/Gene Lee, 23 Alam/Stock Image

Contents

Good for me 4

Protein 6

Meat 8

Fish 10

Farming 12

Buying and storing 14

Cooking meat 16

Eating fish 18

Food chart 20

A balanced diet 22

Glossary 24

Index 24

Good for me

We need to eat food and drink water to live, grow and be **healthy**. All our food comes from animals and plants. Meat and fish are food from animals.

Bulls, cows, sheep, pigs and chickens all give us meat.

Fishing boats catch
fish far out at sea.

Fish are animals that live in
water. Cod, tuna and herring
are fish that live in the sea.
Salmon and trout are river fish.
Meat and fish are delicious to
eat. They are good for you!

5

Protein

Meat and fish are a kind of food called **protein**. Protein helps you to grow and to have strong bones. It helps your body to heal after an accident and to get better after an illness.

Protein gives you **energy** to work and play.

Try to eat at least one **portion** of protein every day. At least one portion of oily fish a week, such as sardines, tuna and salmon, is good for you.

Lunch box

Mix some flakes of smoked mackerel into a salad for a healthy lunch.

White fish with vegetables makes a healthy meal.

7

Meat

Beef, lamb and pork are red meat. Red meat may contain lots of **fat**. Too much fat is unhealthy and not good for you. Cut the fat off meat before you eat it.

Meat like this beef only has a little fat.

Stir-fried chicken breast with vegetables makes a tasty meal that is good for you.

White meat has very little fat. The breast meat of chicken and turkey is white meat. The legs and wings are dark meat. There is fat in the crispy skin of roast chicken.

Lunch box

Roll thin slices of **lean** red meat or chicken around strips of cucumber and spring onion.

Fish

Cod, haddock, plaice, hake and whiting are all white fish. White fish has very little fat when it is baked, grilled or steamed. Fried white fish makes a more fatty meal.

Chunks of white fish can be made into fish kebabs and grilled.

Lunch box

Mash salmon from a tin and spread it onto wholemeal bread for a delicious sandwich.

Oily fish, such as salmon, have more fish oil than white fish.

Trout, salmon, tuna, sardines and herring are oily fish. Fish **oil** is a good kind of fat that helps to keep your brain and heart healthy.

Farming

Farmers raise animals for meat.
Free-range pigs, chickens and turkeys
can run around in a field or yard.
Animals that are not free-range are
kept in barns and pens.

Free-range chickens can wander around
and peck grain from the ground.

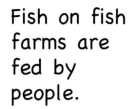

Fish on fish farms are fed by people.

Most of the fish we eat are caught in rivers and lakes or from the sea. Others are raised in specially built fish farms.

Lunch box

Mix flakes of baked fish with cooked rice, a chopped hard-boiled egg and chopped parsley. Eat it cold for lunch.

Buying and storing

Fresh food is good to eat. If it is not fresh it might have **germs** that could make you ill. Store fresh meat and fish in the fridge after you have bought it, and eat it soon.

Fresh meat and fish are delivered to shops and markets every day.

Meat and fish can be frozen, canned or smoked so that they last. Smoked meat and fish stored in the fridge lasts longer than fresh fish.

Lunch box

Fill a wholemeal sandwich with white crab meat from a tin and crispy lettuce.

Frozen fish **fillets** will keep in the freezer for three months.

Cooking meat

Raw meat should be cooked so that it is hot right through to kill any germs. Grills and barbecues are a healthy way to cook meat because any fat drips away.

Barbecues are great for cooking kebabs, fish fillets and steaks.

Curried meat is cooked with spices such as cumin and turmeric.

Lunch box

Make small meatballs with minced meat, herbs and spices. Ask an adult to grill them and eat them cold for lunch.

Cooking meat slowly makes it tender and tasty. Meat cooked slowly in water with vegetables, herbs and spices can be used to make soups, stews and curries.

Eating fish

Fish can be eaten raw and cooked.
Crabs, lobsters and shellfish are **seafood**.
Seafood is usually cooked. Oysters are a
kind of shellfish that are eaten raw with
a squeeze of lemon juice.

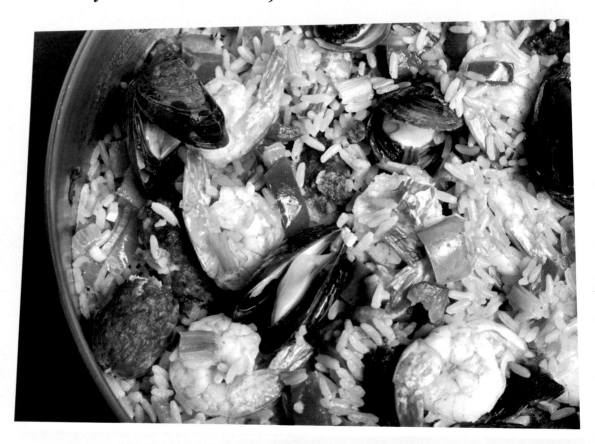

The Spanish dish paella is made
from seafood, chicken and rice.

18

Raw salmon is hung over wood fires and smoked to make smoked salmon.

Lunch box

Mix cold pasta with small pieces of smoked salmon, a little olive oil and a squeeze of lemon juice.

Sushi is a Japanese fish dish made from thin slices of raw fish. This raw fish is dipped into tasty sauces. Raw fish should always be very fresh.

Food chart

Here are some examples of food that can be made using two types of meat and one type of fish. Have you tried any of these?

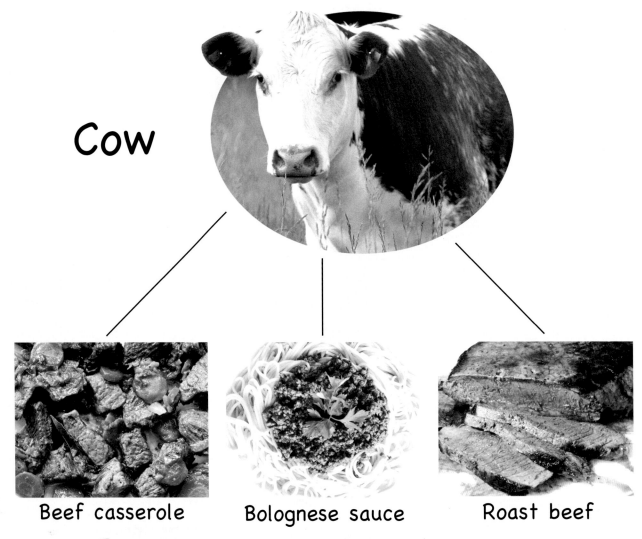

Cow

Beef casserole   Bolognese sauce   Roast beef

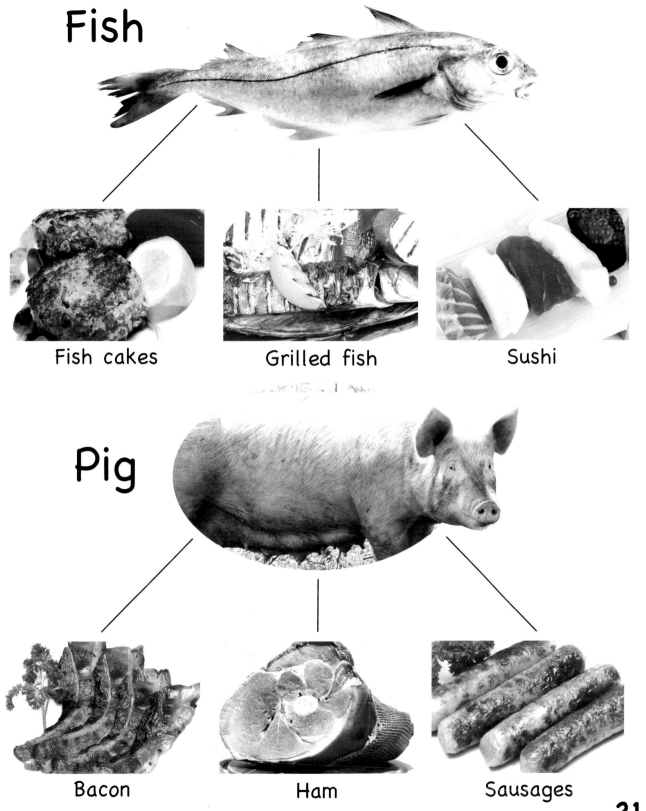

Fish

Fish cakes

Grilled fish

Sushi

Pig

Bacon

Ham

Sausages

A balanced diet

This chart shows you how much you can eat of each food group. The larger the area on the chart, the more of that food group you can eat. For example, you can eat a lot of fruit and vegetables, but only a little oil and sweets. Drink plenty of water every day, too.

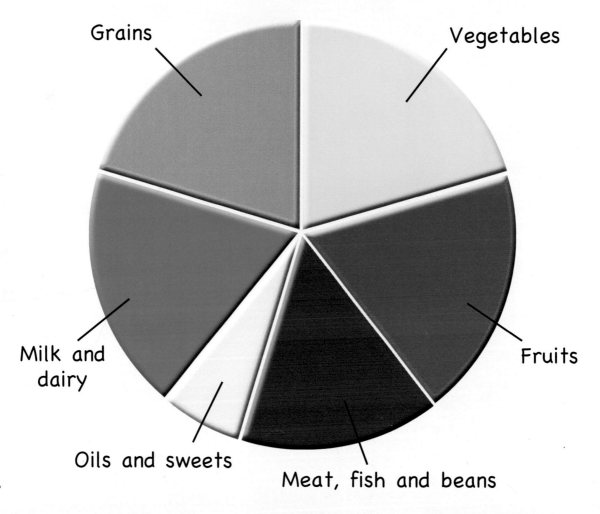

Grains

Vegetables

Milk and dairy

Fruits

Oils and sweets

Meat, fish and beans

Our bodies also need exercise to stay healthy. You should spend at least 20 minutes exercising every day so that your body stays fit and healthy.

Exercising with friends is a fun way to stay fit and healthy.

23

Glossary

Energy The power we need to live and grow.

Fat The white or clear part of meat. You need to eat a little fat to give you energy, but you should not eat too much.

Fillets Pieces of meat or fish with no bones.

Free-range When farm animals can wander in fields or yards and are not kept in pens.

Germs Tiny creatures that can be harmful and can make you ill.

Healthy When you are fit and not ill.

Lean Something that contains very little fat.

Oil A type of fat that is liquid or runny. Oily fish have more fish oil than white fish.

Portion This is the amount of food a person should eat. A child's portion is smaller than an adult's portion.

Protein A type of food that helps you to grow.

Raw Not cooked.

Seafood Food from the sea, including fish, crabs and lobsters.

Index

bacon 21
barbecues 16
beef 8, 20

chicken (meat) 7, 9
chickens 4, 8, 12
cod 5, 10
cows 4, 20

fat 8, 24
fish farms 13
fishing boats 5
free-range animals 12
frozen meat and fish 15

germs 14, 16, 24

haddock 10
hake 10
ham 21
herring 11

kebabs 10, 16

pigs 4, 12, 21
protein 6, 7, 24

raw meat and fish 16, 19, 24

salmon 5, 7, 11, 19
sardines 7, 11
sausages 21
seafood 18, 24
sheep 4
smoked meat and fish 15, 19
sushi 19, 21

trout 5, 11
tuna 5, 7, 11
turkey 9, 12